10 Gifts Your Children
Will Grow to Appreciate

10 Gifts Your Children Will Grow to Appreciate

Lynn P. Clayton

PEAKE ROAD
Macon, Georgia

ISBN 1-57312-174-6

10 Gifts Your Children Will Grow to Appreciate

Lynn P. Clayton

Copyright © 1998
Peake Road

Smyth & Helwys Publishing, Inc.
6316 Peake Road
Macon, Georgia 31210-3960
1-800-747-3016

Library of Congress Cataloging-in-Publication Data

Clayton, Lynn P.
    10 gifts your children will grow to appreciate/
Lynn P. Clayton.
    p.   cm.
    ISBN 1-57312-174-6 (alk. paper)
    1. Child rearing.
    2. Child development.
    3. Child psychology.
    I. Title.
    HQ769.C618 1998
    649'.1—dc21
                                                97-50016
                                                    CIP

Contents

In grateful appreciation to
Ron Parks Clayton and Stephanie Suzanne Clayton
and their Daddy Roy and Gran,
each of whom touched my soul
with many gifts

More Thought Than Things

Brightly colored hunks of wrapping paper lie crumpled around the room. Bows are strewn here and there. Toys that elicited shrieks of thrill and shouts of joy only two hours before are abandoned; they litter the Christmas battle scene. The children are nowhere in sight. The parents sit amidst the mess, too tired from staying up all night getting the gifts ready, and then getting up for good after little Maggie awakened the third time—at 5:30 A.M. They try with less than 100-percent success to hide their frustrations.

"I can't believe it. We shopped every toy store in the area to find this," the father moans, as he holds a talking doll. "We paid that woman who had gotten the last one twice its price just so we could have it this morning. And here it is. The kids couldn't wait to go play with the neighborhood kids' toys. And did you see your daughter? She was dragging that filthy, worn-out thing we bought on sale at Wal-Mart and gave her last year as an afterthought."

"I know. We promised ourselves last Christmas we weren't going to get into this situation this year, and here we are again," the mother agrees. "We spent more on gifts this year than we did last year, and they got up and out of here earlier than they did last year. About the only thing that will make this a memorable Christmas is that our credit card payments will be larger and will take longer to pay."

"I guess all we can do is try," the dad sighs. "But next year let's try to give the kids something they will appreciate, not just what they want. This is getting old."

Every parent has been there, and not just at Christmas. The parents of young children aren't the only ones who struggle to give gifts their children will appreciate. A friend tells of an experience with his young-adult children.

The middle-aged parents leave on Sunday morning, before even the early bird has cracked an eye, and drive a considerable distance to the home of one of their daughters who lives in another state. They perform a number of tasks that parents do for adult children—tasks the younger generation could do, but don't because they know they can "get Mother and Daddy to do it." You know, tasks that are too much trouble, too time-consuming, and too expensive for the kids to do themselves. The younger couple watches as the parents get the things done. The mother quickly throws together sandwiches for the road, and off the parents go again.

My friend and his wife then drive hard to get to the next daughter's home in still another state. There they perform even more parental acts of love.

Late that night they make the long drive home so they can be at their own jobs early the next morning. Driving along that midnight road, Ken asks his wife longingly, "Do you think they appreciate what we give them and what we do for them?"

The wife thinks carefully and then answers, "Not now they don't." In her wisdom, the mother knows her children are not appreciative now, but she holds on to honest hope that one day they will be. Maybe she draws more from her experience as an offspring than as a mother.

Having hope that one day our children will appreciate what we give them is the case concerning much about being a parent. Parenting is generally the most unappreciated job this side of divine grace. We give and give, and we sacrifice and give, but our children remain steadfastly unappreciative. The depth of their thanks, when it comes, in no way matches the depth of our giving nor the value of the gifts.

My father's frequent exhortation still rings in my memory: "The least you kids can do is thank your mother and be grateful for all she does, especially what she does around here for you. She works hard around here all day long, and you kids just come in and clutter and never help and never say thank-you." Sometimes, in the midst of these well-worn speeches to his three offspring, one got the feeling he wanted a little appreciation, too. Can you imagine?

We never really understood the intensity of his frustration. We-three-kings just didn't see that providing our food, clothing, shelter, entertainment, and medical care was all that big a deal. After all, wasn't she our mother? Wasn't he our father? Wasn't that what mothers do? Wasn't that what fathers do? And didn't we follow our training by thanking her for the good meal every time we excused ourselves from the table? And didn't we say "thanks" when Daddy gave us money? Geez, what's the big deal?

The bottom line is, parents have to give a lot to get a little from their children. And often, we have to give tremendously to get just a "thanks" spoken hastily over the shoulder as they run out the door.

Receiving appreciation from our children is usually like mining for gold. The miners go deeply into the mountain, blasting and digging. They move tons and tons of muck, and then haul out the gold-laden ore. The ore is refined, and the gold is separated from the encasing rock. Finally, out of all those tons of rock, the miners are able to extract a few ounces of gold. Certainly any words of thanks or appreciation from our children are as precious as that gold!

Ah, but there is hope. There is hope that one day our children will appreciate the truly significant gifts we have given them. They may never appreciate the ten months of payments we made on those material gifts given at Christmas. But, if we give them the right kinds of gifts, there is a wonderful chance they will appreciate them when they are older. The trick is to give children the right kinds of gifts and then manage to live long enough to see their gratitude!

This book is about gifts you can give to your children that they will grow to appreciate. Living long enough to experience that gratitude is up to you and your genes. If your children are teenagers or younger, they probably will not appreciate these gifts for a decade or longer. They may even fight you tooth and nail to keep from getting them. But one day it could happen.

These gifts will not seem all that important to them now. But one day your children will be older, and maybe even wiser, and they will see the unsurpassing value of what you have given them. If they have been appreciative earlier, their appreciation will deepen.

Note, if you give all the gifts mentioned in this book, you will not be a perfect parent, and your children will not see you as a perfect parent. Giving these gifts to your children will not mean your children will be perfect, and they may not even turn out "right," which usually means to turn out exactly the way you want them. Nothing guarantees that. These gifts do not mean you will not have problems with your children. Hey, this isn't a magic book. But these ten gifts are precious gifts your children will appreciate when they are older because each gift gives your children something with eternal value—each gift touches their souls.

Each gift is grounded in two realities, Scripture and my own life. First, I have tried not to come up with my own ideas and then run to the Bible to see if I can find some kind of verse that backs up what I say. Okay, so maybe I did that a couple of times, but mostly I have found the principle somewhere in the Bible and included it on the list. Or maybe I discovered the principle and realized that the Bible speaks to it directly or indirectly a number of times. I have included these principles in my discussions of the gifts. Either way, you will see what I mean. But I have tried to include only gifts that have their reality in Scripture.

Second, I base my ideas on what I have experienced and observed. My list of gifts includes the things my parents gave me that are the most meaningful to me or that I wish they had given me in greater measure. They are things I have given my two children or, more likely, wish I had given in greater abundance. One thing for sure, the two children God entrusted to my household are not shy when it comes to telling me things I should have done better!

I have seen the reality of these gifts, or the lack of them, in the lives of other people. I have seen great need for these gifts in the lives of children and seen the voids in adults because they did not receive them. I also have seen the remarkable results of these gifts in the strong character of their recipients.

These guidelines to giving assume that parents are Christians who want to see their children accept Christ as Savior and grow up to be responsible people who are involved in the life of a church. Certainly the most important gift parents can give their children is an example of a redeemed life and the opportunities to hear the gospel and accept Christ as personal Savior. Nothing can replace these gifts, but in this little book, they are a given.

You might think none of the gifts mentioned here are startling or new. I thought I would say that before you thought it. But I hope they will serve all of us parents as sort of a refresher course on giving our children what is truly important in life.

Hopefully, both mother and dad will read this book and discuss each gift. Give yourself a checkup on how you are doing in giving your children the gifts that matter most. If you are really brave, you can let your kids give you a checkup on how you are doing. I strongly encourage this. You may be amazed by how much these things mean to your children. They certainly will let you know how you can improve! (I've taken the test, and I steadfastly refuse to share my score!)

After all, when I'm old and gray (like I'm not now!), on a cold winter's eve, I want one of my two children to call up and say, "You know, Dad, I was thinking about (pick one of the ten gifts), and I gotta tell you, I may have thought it was dumb then, but I really appreciate it now. It has made a positive difference in my life. Thank-you."

If I have learned anything, I will say simply, "Thank-you," and I will be glad I'm on the phone so my tears of gratitude will not show.

The Magic of Touch

What a scene! We had moved to a new community, and I managed to make the high school football team.

I gloried in being a really rough, tough 165-pound defensive middle guard. My father and my brother before me made their teams, and by the skin of my teeth, I made mine. One thing about small schools, even a 165-pound lineman can make the team.

We football players had gathered, ready to board the bus for our first road trip to a rival school ten miles away. My dad was there, talking to everyone, encouraging the players, probably reliving his past. Embarrassing!

Then, as I was getting ready to take that first step up in manhood and into the bus, my dad came over. Right there in front of God and every teenager in America, he hugged me and told me he loved me and hoped I had a good game.

I wanted to die on the spot, but I was starting at defensive middle guard that night. I made all kinds of faces, hoping it would restore my manhood. I walked down the school bus aisle and plopped onto the seat beside our 275-pound offensive tackle.

"I can't stand it when he does that," I said in disgust

The huge mountain stunned me. "I don't know why. I would give anything if my dad would do that."

In the brief discussion that followed, the roughest, toughest, meanest senior in town told me how his father and mother never hugged him or told him they loved him, and how much he longed for the day when they would. All I could say was, "Really?" Right then and there, as a high school junior on the way to play football, I was thankful for my parents' gift—and I have been ever since.

Sort of strange that at a time when many studies indicate the importance of showing love physically to our children, we are in the midst of child-abuse awareness. Hopefully, the abuse awareness grows from understanding the importance of proper physical love.

A television program a couple of years ago pointed out the strategic need children have for love expressed in physical ways. The report told about prematurely birthed babies. Some of the babies shown on the program were tiny; some weighed no more than three or four pounds. They could have been held in the palm of a grown-up hand.

Doctors told the television reporter that one of the greatest needs of preemies is physical contact—for caring, loving touches from their parents. Yet, the parents of the babies shown on the program did not feel free to pick up their infants and love them due to the babies' tiny sizes and frail conditions and the needles and tubes protuding from their bodies. The doctors finally told the parents that unless they overcame their trepidations and held the babies and gave them physical love, the babies were not as likely to continue living, improving, and growing.

Since that report was televised, there has been coverage of hospitals that have a large number of abandoned babies. These hospitals enlist volunteers to come into the infant wards and hold these parentless babies and express physical love to them. The holding and showing of physical love make an unbelievable difference on the well-being in every area of the children's lives.

Now, I am no psychologist, nor am I the son of a psychologist, but I think I can say with little fear of contradiction by mental health folks: healthy, caring, nurturing physical expressions of love are vital to the well-being of children of all ages. In fact, all God's children need healthy, caring, nurturing physical expressions of love—even guys old enough to be grandads!

I speak to singles groups fairly regularly, and I usually tell them: "I have heard that everyone needs from three to eight hugs a day from another person to maintain emotional well-being. I think some psychiatrist came up with the three hugs idea, and some lonely single jumped the number to eight. Now, I don't know if that is true or not, but if it is true, that is one of the reasons some of you are so crazy—you aren't getting your share of the hugs." Then I pause and have everyone give/receive at least one hug and more if they can get them. I tell the singles: "Now I know there are right kinds of hugs and wrong kinds of hugs. There are wholesome hugs and some pretty creepy hugs. But don't run from all hugs just because some creepy, sick people go around hugging all wrong. Avoid those creepy huggers, and hug the wholesome huggers—unless, of course, the creepy hugger is your fiancé. In that case, see me after the meeting, and I will help you get some counseling."

If you need further convincing about the importance of showing physical love, just check your Bible. In the Bible, there are strong images and word pictures of God as a Father showing love to His children in physical ways, drawing them to His breast, holding them, caressing them. The Scriptures picture God as holding His children protectively and lovingly in the palm of His hand. God is pictured even as a mother suckling Her children.

In his earthly ministry, Jesus constantly expressed his love in healing power. Frequently, when he demonstrated his loving, healing power, he did it by physically reaching out and touching. This touch was more than just a calculated point of contact. It was reaching out and touching people who probably had not been touched in a pure, loving way for years.

- He touched those who could not reach out and touch anyone.
- He touched those whom no one would reach out and touch.
- He touched the lepers.
- He touched the lady ceremoniously defiled by an issue of blood.
- He touched the prostitute who had been touched only in a lustful manner.

Can you imagine how wonderful Jesus' touch must have been to those who had seen people running away to keep from touching them?

This business of showing your children healthy physical love—just plain old holding and hugging—is high on the list of gifts your children will enjoy now and thank you for one day.

My parents were an interesting pair when it came to showing physical love. My father was physically demonstrative in just about every way. Dad believed in extending this "physical" all the way to punishment. He also showed his love physically. I can remember as a child sitting on my father's lap as he watched television and feeling great security there. When bedtime came, he would give me a kiss and send me off to my room. I can still remember feeling his beard stubble on my face.

As a pre-adolescent, I knew that when I awoke and walked out of my room into the kitchen for breakfast, if my father were there, I would get a hug and a kiss on the cheek. It was a secure way to start the day.

On many nights when I was an older teenager, Dad and I roamed the streets of the small towns where we lived, searching out other night owls. We would be standing there, talking to the insomniacs of our little world, and Dad would put his arm around me and give me a sideways squeeze and say, "Yes sir, this is my boy." Funny, when I looked in a mirror right after that, I was amazed I didn't look nearly as tall as I felt.

Parental hugs and cheek kisses were part of my growing-up years. My dad, ever the macho man, let my brother and me know that men, such as ourselves, only kissed on the cheek. And you only hugged your dad, but certainly manly father-son hugs were right and good.

An interesting sidelight on this business of parents and children hugging . . . My mother was never a physically demonstrative person. The hugs and kisses she offered were generally few, and those usually came after we had gone to bed and she had read us a Bible story. (I'll tell you a secret. This saintly pastor's wife sometimes skipped the Bible story and read to us from Mark Twain's *Huckleberry Finn*. I liked them both.)

One day in Sunday School our teacher asked us, "When is the last time you went up to your mother and gave her a hug and told her you loved her?" Then she challenged us to do that "today, when your mother is cooking dinner." (Guess that dates me!) There was no more dependable fact than that my mother would be cooking Sunday dinner, which is at noon in my part of the world.

Well, I waited until Mother had donned her apron and was at the kitchen counter preparing the meal. I walked over to her and, with great determination and some hesitation, without warning, gave Mother a super-duper hug, kissed her firmly on the cheek, looked her in the eyes, and said, "I love you."

Startled the poor thing! But, when she regained her composure, she said, "Thank you."

I asked, "Is my doing that okay?"

She smiled and said, "Lynn, I love it when you hug me and tell me that."

Well, I started doing it right regular and continued through the minute life passed from her tiny body. Those hugs were important to her and therefore gifts to me. In the last years of her life, when I walked into her room at the nursing home, she would do the best she could to hold up her arthritic arms and say, "Give your mother a hug, you big lug." Those kinds of moments are gifts for which I will ever be grateful.

Hug your children abundantly, whatever age they are—even if you have a teenage daughter, which I just survived, who finds getting a hug from her father only slightly less repulsive than being hugged by the class nerd. Give her a hug. Maybe not in front of every other teenager in America, but give her a hug. She will get over her disgust of being hugged just like she will get over being a teenager.

Right now some of you, especially men, are saying that you just can't freely show physical affection. You weren't brought up that way. You want to, you say, but you just can't do it. Balderdash! You have overcome all other kinds of emotional difficulties, and you can overcome that hang-up, too. Just start, and the more you hug your kids, the more you will like it and the more it will mean to you. Even if it isn't easy at first, do it.

And some of you older parents need to make up for some lost hugging. It is never too late this side of the grave. Show your kids physical love, and maybe, just maybe, you will live long enough to hear them say: "You know, back when I was a kid and you hugged me and told me you loved me, I thought you were the most old-fashioned person in town. But now I think that was just about the neatest thing you ever did." And maybe, just maybe, you will forget about that dust-covered, long-abandoned $1,500 guitar you gave the kid at age thirteen, after hearing for a year that he/she was going to be the next Rock-A-Belly-Jelly earning $5 trillion a year.

Being Cherished Unconditionally

There I was sitting at graduation party #8. It seems every high school senior needs at least a dozen nowadays. Those of us family members who were privileged to attend sat in the shade while the seniors swam and played volleyball. Among those sitting in the shade was one half of a family—a daughter and a mother whose only son was graduating. The daughter was in her mid-twenties and about to be married in six weeks.

The daughter was tall, strikingly beautiful, and loaded with personality. The father was not present because he and the mother had divorced several years earlier. It had not been an amicable parting, and both had been through second marriages. Amazingly, with people sitting around whom they hardly knew, the mother and daughter started reminiscing about the interrelationship of the girl's father, mother, and brother.

"Grandma says I am just like my mother. It's true. I'm just like my mother," the daughter said. "Exactly like her. And my brother is just like my daddy. I mean just like him —just a younger version. And my daddy knows it, and that's why he can't stand me. He got to where he couldn't stand Mother, and that's why he divorced her, right Mother? I guess he would divorce me if he could. I guess the reason he loves my brother so much is because it's just like loving himself."

The young lady was speaking with great humor, but no one hearing her talk doubted her feelings. There she was facing a marriage with that kind of "tape" playing in her head.

"Is she right?" I asked the mother.

The mother paused thoughtfully and answered, "I never thought about it until recently when her relationship with her father came up in a premarital counseling session. I asked her father about it. He admitted that her personality being so much like mine might be a major factor in their not getting along."

Another time I witnessed the public confrontation of a mother and her thirteen-year-old daughter. It was not a pretty sight. The daughter loudly voiced her disagreement with her mother, and she would not "let it go." She kept coming back with a comment as her mother calmly tried to reason with her. Finally, the teenager turned to walk away and gave one parting shot.

The mother was embarrassed. She had three other children, and I had never seen one of them act confrontational or rude to their parents or to anyone else. Usually, the daughter who had just bucked her mother was a nice, polite kid.

After the daughter and her entourage marched out of the room, the mother took a deep breath, looked over at me, and said, "Let's face it. Some kids are easier to love than others."

There is no reason to put the mother on trial because of one statement made in exasperation after a difficult moment with her strong-willed daughter. Actually, most of us parents who witnessed the confrontation thought the mother's statement was extremely controlled and mild! But in frustration, the mother said what many parents might not admit but know and prove by their actions: some children are easier to love than others.

A father told me about an experience he and his wife had with a counselor. The subject of the session was the father's relationship with his children, with which the mother was not pleased. For several minutes the mother told of the dad's failures as a father. The mother was especially harsh on the father's relationship with their son. The father admitted he and his son did not get along and then tried to justify his relationship with his son by pointing out the mother's failure.

The counselor listened intently. Then he asked the father, "What about your daughter? Do you get along with her?"

"Oh, I have a great relationship with her," the father was proud to say after taking such a beating about his relationship with his son.

The wife quickly rejoined, "So what? She gets along with everyone," implying his good relationship with his daughter was a credit to her, not the dad.

The dad said the counselor responded, "Oh, she's easy [to get along with]."

Anyone who knows the brother and the sister knows that she is easy to know and to maintain a relationship with. The dad liked his daughter and enjoyed her friendship more, and it showed. He did not like his son as well, and that showed too.

The entire business of human personality is a fascinating subject and an ongoing industry. But it seems no one can explain why some children have pleasant personalities and others just seem to be argumentative and difficult. As the mother said, some children just seem easier to love than others, even when they are your own flesh and blood. Saying one of our children may be easier than another to love sounds horrible, but in many cases it is true. You might as well admit it as a beginning point to correcting the problem.

The Bible does not give options on loving our children; it reveals a command: "Parents, love your children." Because this is a command, it can be done. We are to love not just the children who are easy to love, but each and every one of our children.

Because this is a command, it is a matter of will, not emotions. That's where most of us make a major mistake. We think that loving and cherishing our children is a matter of emotion— something we do if and when we feel like it. It should first be a matter of will. Cherishing our children, and helping them to feel cherished, is a choice. It is something we decide to do and therefore do.

You can believe it: Children know how we feel about them, even if we do not admit it to ourselves. I tease my sister about my parents' attitude toward her, especially my mother's. "You were, after all, Mother's favorite." Now that we are both old enough to be grandparents, she will admit she was. Our parents were not able to hide their affections for their children, and we are not able to hide ours from our children.

No child should have to go through life knowing, or feeling as if, he is not loved and cherished by the father or mother who brought him into the world. Let me explain what the word cherished means in the context of this writing. It's like a pastor once told me, "I can believe God loves me, but I cannot conceive of Him liking me." Some parents may let their kids know they "love" them, but they fail to communicate that they "like" them and cherish them.

I am using the word cherish to get us to think about our relationship with our children without using words that have a lot of emotional baggage. Cherish means to hold dear, to care for tenderly, to nurture, to hold in our minds, to think fondly of a person. It means that even if our children were not our children, we would cherish them. It means that our affection goes beyond obligation or blood relation.

All parents seem to have an emotional attachment to their children. Even parents who have never seen their children and are suddenly united with them—sometimes when the children are adults—express a great emotional attachment to them. But these parents have not given their offspring a sense of being cherished.

Through the years I have had the opportunity of leading a number of seminars for single parents. One of the most common cries of single mothers is, "How can I get my children's father to spend more time with them?"

In trying to help these single mothers cope with this desperate need, I quickly discover that most of these fathers spent little time with their children when they lived with the family. If I ask the missing father, "Do you love your children?" he is insulted that I would even ask. If I ask him why he does not spend time with his children, he reveals that while he may love them in some sort of deficient way, he does not cherish them nor their presence.

Dads often have more difficulty showing their more tender emotions. They will yell and scream and shout with joy and moan and gripe at football games, but they are intimidated by the thought of expressing tender love to their children. Even modern-day men struggle with it. But what a great hole dads leave in their children's lives if they do not let them feel the deep emotion of being cherished.

A friend of mine often told me of his father whom he greatly admired. His father was a real outdoorsman who allowed his son to spend hours with him fishing and hunting. While his father gave him great gifts of time, he did not give him the freedom to show any emotion. I guess as kids we all had a few experiences watching our parents that made deep impressions on us about what it means to be a man or a woman. For this son, the experience came when the father came upon a deer swimming in a river in a deep Louisiana swamp. The father pulled his boat along the struggling deer and killed it in a rather brutal fashion.

"He showed absolutely no emotion, no feeling, just a cold-bloodedness. I used that as my lesson on how men who are in control do things."

The boy grew up, married, and became the father of two girls and a boy. But he dealt with his wife and children in a cold, unfeeling, unemotional manner. He tells his story:

> My dad showed me a lot of wonderful things, but he never showed me how to feel or to show feelings. My wife left me because she said she never felt loved, never felt cherished. I lost my kids, too. They feel the same way toward me as their mother feels.
>
> Now I'm trying to learn how to deal with the pain I feel. I'm trying to learn how to tell my wife, my ex-wife now, and my kids how much I love and cherish them. Maybe I'm at the first phase because I've never felt so much pain in my life. I cry now and never thought I could do that.
>
> My son is twenty-one, and I'm trying to learn how to show him how much I love him, and how proud I am of him, and how I really want to be friends with him. I can't believe I never told him these things before. I pray to God He gives me enough chances with my son to convince him of these things.
>
> You know, I wonder if my dad loved me. He never said he did. I wonder if he just took me along to have someone to help him, or if he liked me and wanted to be with me. I'll never know. He died two years ago, and I could never bring myself to ask him. I guess I couldn't stand the thought of a negative answer. And now, I think about my son not knowing how much I love him and really like him . . . I can't fail at that. And then, there are my daughters . . .

How terribly sad, but how hopeful that the son who was not given the sense of being cherished may now be able to give his son the gift of being cherished.

It seems to me a wonderful case can be made that the greatest gift God gives each person is his or her personality. The New Testament term for soul is *psyche* from which we build the English words psychology and psychiatry. Psychiatry means the healing of the soul. Soul is the essence of our being—it is who we are. When the Bible talks about saving the soul, it is not talking about some disembodied spirit, but about the essence of who we are. Our psyche is everything we are emotionally, physically, and spiritually.

God gives every person this psyche. Each person is more than a compilation of his parents' genes and chromosomes. Each person is more than a product of her environment. These elements contribute to a person's personality and behavior, but each person is more. Each person is a creation of God. God's plan for our lives includes becoming our best selves—our redeemed selves. The cliché "Be patient, God isn't finished with me yet" is true. We can never rest, saying, "This is who I am." We are always becoming, and we are gifting our children so they can become more like God's goal for them.

If children feel cherished for this psyche, they can venture forward in life, determined to make the best of who they are, while eliminating the negatives that keep them from being their best and doing their best. Children feel cherished when . . .

• they have a sense of being dear to their parents
• they know their parents enjoy being with them
• they know their parents appreciate them for who they are
• their parents affirm their character, personality, and positive values
• their parents encourage them to be their best selves
• their parents do not compare them to others.

The gift of being cherished is appreciated immediately by children, but they grow to appreciate it even more as they grow older.

Be alert for ways you can affirm your children, who they are as well as what they do. When one of your children does something you think is right, or good, or noble, try to look below the surface of that action to the nature of the child that sparked the action. For example, "John, I saw the way you helped Bill when he was being picked on. I think you showed your sense of fairness, and I want to tell you I was proud of you."

A newspaper ran a feature article about a highly successful, greatly admired lawyer. In that article the reporter related a story the lawyer had told him. When the lawyer was five, his grandfather was teaching him how to drive a horse pulling a plow. The grandfather explained to the lad the importance of holding on to the reigns that controlled the horse. The boy was practicing when the plow horse, apparently sensing a novice, broke and ran across the pasture. Remembering his grandfather's exhortation to always hold the reigns, he hung on tenaciously as the horse ran across the field. The horse stopped when he reached the fence, and the grandfather was able to run to the horse. When he got there, the boy was beaten, scraped, scratched, and cut from being dragged through the brush and over the rocks. But he still held the reigns. "My grandfather said that episode didn't speak well of my intelligence, but it did speak well of my determination." The story became part of the bonding the grandson enjoyed with his grandfather. He felt cherished by his grandfather. His grandfather's rather two-edged comment instilled in the then-small boy a sense that he could, by determination, achieve. And did he.

When I was a senior in high school and played football, our team experienced a heartbreaking defeat. I left the dressing room knowing I would have to face my father, a former football player who could be a harsh critic of my play. I walked toward the car with him and told him of my disappointment. He put his arm around me and said: "Son, I know you are disappointed with the loss, and the team is important. But if everyone had played as you played tonight, you would have won. Even though you lost, I was proud of you. You played hard every down, including the last one. There are some things more important than winning." That night a special feeling of appreciation was placed in my heart that stayed with me through many difficult days, times when I did not win but knew I did my best.

So, help your children to feel cherished for who they are. They may not have to be much older before they appreciate it.

Listening, Then Disciplining

When I was in the third grade, we lived in the tiny parsonage of a tiny congregation in a tiny town on the vast Texas plains. The size of Dad's salary matched the size of the parsonage, congregation, and town—not the vast plains. We were fortunate, however, because he was able to supplement our income by working at the cotton gin during harvest time.

Mother must have had Daddy well-trained. He would get his check, go to the bank where he cashed it, and then bring the cash home to her. She would put the money in the top drawer of a chest of drawers and then make meager withdrawals from the stash throughout the week. She watched that money like a hawk because when it was gone, all the money we had was gone.

One morning I noticed Mother was going through the house, obviously searching for something. Actually, the task could not have been that great because there were only two bedrooms, a living room, and a kitchen, and the rooms were sparsely furnished. But she diligently searched and researched every nook and cranny.

As the day wore on, Mother's frantic searching and researching grew more intense. Dad was gone, and she had no one to help her. Something of major importance was missing.

She finally called my older brother and me to her and said, "Boys, I must ask you if either of you bothered the money that was in the top drawer."

I told her, "No ma'am."

My brother answered, "No ma'am."

"If one of you has, please tell me," and the tears began to well up in her eyes. "It's all we have, and Daddy is gone."

I felt terrible, but I had not taken the money.

Late that night I awakened to earnest sobs. I looked from my top bunk into the adjoining kitchen and saw my brother sobbing in his mother's arms. She was comforting him with reassuring words. He had taken the money. Why? Who knows? Who knows why twelve-year-olds do most of the things they do? But his guilt and pain had become so great as he lay in bed trying to escape into sleep, he could no longer stand it. He got up, went outside, retrieved the money from his secret hiding place, and brought it to Mother.

Well, my brother was four years older and considerably larger than I, and he could always get the best of me in any skirmish. One of the few joys I had concerning him was when he would get a spanking. I just knew that for committing such a terrible act Mother would "beat the daylights out of him." But she didn't.

I was mad. Why didn't she spank him? The next morning I sulked.

Finally Mother came to me, put her arm around me, and asked, "What's wrong, Honey?"

"It's Paul. I can't believe what he did. And then, as terrible as it was, you didn't spank him. Why didn't you wear him out for what he did? Daddy would have torn up Paul's britches."

Her answer that morning, thousands of mornings ago, is as real this morning as it was when she spoke them.

"Honey, what Paul did was wrong, terribly wrong. But what he needed last night was not a spanking. What he needed last night was love."

I have no idea what that episode meant to Paul; I never asked him. But I do know what an impact it had on me and how much I learned that day. I have never forgotten it. I regret there were times I acted in anger and haste toward my children before I remembered the wonderful lesson my mother lived that night: There are times for punishing, but there should be time for listening and understanding.

My parents were good parents. And they got better every day. Actually, they started getting better right after I left home to follow the wheat harvest after my senior year in high school. They improved while I was in college, grew even better while I was in seminary, and blossomed into brilliant by the time my first child was three years old. Now, having survived two children of my own making it to adulthood, I contemplate my folk's parental skills, and they geyser into marvelous. (I don't know that I would have voted for my parents to be in "The Parents Hall of Fame" until my first child hit ten years of age. Yes, he hit ten like he hits just about everything else—he shattered it!)

A part of their parenting expertise was the threat and delivery of spankings. They were really good at it. In those days—looked upon condescendingly as barbaric by today's child-rearing know-it-alls—spanking was considered the court of first, second, third, last, and all-in-between resort. Enthusiastic spanking was a standard part of child rearing in our part of the world, and my parents participated. Yes sir, my parents believed in corporal punishment for their children. In fact, there were times I thought they believed in capital punishment for my brother, my sister, and me!

Mother was a slight thing, and my brother and I were larger than she by the time we were thirteen. One day, my brother—four years older than I—made the horrible mistake of laughing while mother administered a spanking. From that point on, she handed off all corporal punishment to Dad.

On those extremely rare occasions we drove mother to distraction or committed a major disobedience, she would announce, "When your Daddy gets home, I am going to have him spank you." We would spend the rest of the day in angelic repose, hoping she would change her mind or "forget" to tell the executioner. We discovered that Mother had the patience of a saint, but when we crossed the line, she was as resolute in her threats as we had been in our misbehavior.

I suppose I needed every spanking I got. At least my parents told me I needed every spanking I got, and more! There were even times, after a quickly-administered spanking, I was able to convince my parents that I had not been the one "who started it." On those occasions my folks would say, "Well, you may not have needed that spanking, but there were others you should have gotten that you didn't get. This one just puts you even."

What can I say?

I'm thankful for my parents' strict discipline. Thinking back, however, I'm not 100-percent sure spankings got their desired message across, except for the fear and pain they elicited. Physical discipline has its place, but many times parents are too quick to resort to spanking because spanking does not call for great reasoning or preparation; it is immediate.

To clear the record, let me say as emphatically as possible, no parent has any business abusing his or her child. No child should be struck in anger or haste. No child should suffer to alleviate the frustration of a parent. Any parent who abuses a child in such a way should run, not walk, to the nearest counselor. Kids are not for hitting. So, what is a parent to do when a child misbehaves and/or disobeys?

You are not going to get my advice on the best way to discipline a child. Happily, that will be left to the experts, of whom there are plenty of self-confessed ones. Rather, I will address the issue of giving your children the gift of understanding before, during, and after disciplining—however you choose to do that.

The Bible speaks clearly that parents are to discipline their children. Proverbs 29 states it brilliantly:

> The rod and reproof give wisdom, but a mother is disgraced by a neglected child. . . Discipline your children, and they will give you rest, they will delight to your heart. (vv. 15, 17)

Solomon, known for his wisdom, wrote these words. Of course, he had the direct help of the Holy Spirit, so he should have said it well. But I wish he had stated as clearly how to correct, and how long it will be before they give you rest and delight your soul. Personally, my parental soul could use a little rest and delight.

Whatever else this correction or discipline is, it is not abruptly yanking a child up and spanking the daylights out of her every time she does something wrong or you think she has done something wrong. Nor is it abruptly grounding a child for being impulsive. When we discipline in this manner, I strongly suspect the pain and suffering we inflict upon a child is more for our benefit than his. At least the spanking vents our anger and helps satisfy our driving desire to do something—anything—to think the situation is not beyond our control. After all, we are the parents, and we are supposed to be able to handle our children. Never mind that fast-draw discipline builds more anger and resentment than understanding and improvement.

A recent study shows that parents who spank their children are provoking the very misbehavior they are trying to stop. But the "boomerang" effect isn't seen by the parents because it happens over weeks or months. Other studies link spanking with increased aggressiveness in children. "Many people, probably most people, believe that if spanking is done by warm and loving parents, it has no harmful side effects, because kids know it's for their own good. That turns out not to be true," said the man who conducted the study. He concludes the study by saying spanking's results are long-term.

As children get older, our discipline becomes less physical but may still display destructive expressions of quick-flash anger. If we can handle our anger and temper when the children are younger than 11, we are likely to go to pieces when they hit adolescence. Makes me think of the scripture, "If you have raced with men on foot and they have worn you out, how can you compete with horses?" (Jer 12:5). I've got news for those of you whose children have reached puberty: The horses are coming, the horses are coming!

Someone once asked me, "Do you know why I know that God waited until Isaac was 28 years old before God told Abraham to offer him as a sacrifice?" I dutifully answered no. "Because if God had told Abraham to kill Isaac when he was 15, it would not have been a sacrifice."

The Bible has some things to say about anger and also about discipline.

- "And the Lord said, 'Is it right for you to be angry?' " (Jonah 4:4).
- "A harsh word stirs up anger" (Prov 15:1).
- "Be slow to anger" (Prov 15:18).
- "One given to anger stirs up strife, and the hothead causes much transgression" (Prov 29:22).
- "For as pressing milk produces curds, and pressing the nose produces blood, so pressing anger produces strife" (Prov 30:33).
- "Fathers, do not provoke your children to anger; but bring them up in the discipline and instruction of the Lord" (Eph 6:4).
- "Fathers, do not provoke your children, or they may lose heart" (Col 3:21).

We hear and/or read these verses but generally think they are in force everywhere except our homes. But the home is where they should be implemented more than anywhere else.

Out of this profound truth the idea for this gift of listening before disciplining grows. Give your ear to your children more than your hand. In other words, strive to really hear and understand what they say moreso than using your hand to punish them. Listen more than spank. Strive to let your correction be the kind that builds understanding in the child about the principles involved. Punishment is important in child rearing, but wise discipline involves more than using our hand to inflict some kind of pain on a child. (And to you yellers out there, let me assure you what yelling accomplishes. Yelling begets yelling. Yelling dulls communication. Besides, it bothers your neighbors.)

Take time to listen carefully. Listen with your heart, and be understanding of your children. Be more intent upon understanding where your children are rather than flying off the handle and using your hand on them to relieve your frustration and anger.

There are times for punishing, but there should always be time for understanding. According to the *Interpreter's Dictionary of the Bible*, in the Bible, "discipline is closely associated with training, instruction and knowledge on the one hand, and with reproof, correction and punishment on the other hand."

It seems to me the purpose of punishment is to teach children to discipline themselves. Children need to understand the "why" of the "do's and don'ts." The only thing parents can hope for is that when the children grow older, they will remember what the parents taught them and then follow that teaching.

Unified Guidance and Discipline

"Stay in the car. I'm going to run in and get some breath mints so I will not blast everyone with coffee breath. I will be right back."

Five-year-old Rob began revving up his engine as he frantically started trying to unfasten his seat belt. He emitted a noise somewhere between that of a fire engine and a jet racing down a runway.

"Oh, Daddy. Don't be that way," said Mom. "It's not going to hurt anything if he goes in with you. Let him go."

"Look, we are running late already," Dad fired back. "He can never just go in and go out. Bible study starts in five minutes, and this is the first chance we've had to be on time in three years."

Dad was suspended half out of the car, and Mom was leaning forward into the front seat as they entered "significant dialogue." Rob's little head bounced back and forth like a tennis match spectator's as he watched the debate. He knew he had 'em going again. He smiled to himself, knowing his way was only a step away.

"Okay, I don't have time to argue. Rob, come on. But you stay with me like a sandspur on a sock. And don't, do not, stop to look at anything else."

Rushing into the convenience store, Dad shot a right to the gum and mints rack. Rob took a hard left to the comic book rack. And why not? Only seconds before he was told he could not get out of the car, and here he was out of the car.

"Daddy, I want this."

"I told you to stay right with me and not to ask for anything."

"I want this comic book."

Dad paid for the mints. Rob, seeing his chance for a comic book fade, revved his engine again. The kid was good at this—real good. But then, practice makes perfect.

Dad grabbed Rob by the arm with one hand and put the comic book back on the shelf with the other. Rob's amazing noise-making machine was at top range. Dad tried to ignore the half dozen sets of inquiring eyes.

Rob blubbered a litany of charges at Dad, beginning with, "Why are you so mean to me?" Dad pled innocent in a rumbling volume, trying to override Rob's noise. (You know the old trick: if you can't outreason 'em, outyell 'em.)

Precious little eighteen-month-old Maggie, who had been sleeping sweetly and unnoticed, awakened in time to join the chorus from her infant seat. Mom, well prepared, rose to the moment and joined by demanding to know what had gone wrong. The choir at church might sound better, but it would not have this quartet's volume.

Dad slammed the door as he slammed the car into reverse. Heads jerked forward. Dad slammed on the breaks. Heads jerked backward. Dad slammed the car into drive and then slammed the pedal to the metal. Heads jerked backward. The whiplashes gave Dad the split-second he needed to squeeze off his ultimate verbal shot.

"I'm going to punish you when we get home."

"Oh, Daddy, why are you being so mean?" Mom pled. "He doesn't need to be punished. He is just a little boy."

Rob cut his eyes to Dad to see if there was hope. He was only five, but he knew this scenario well. If his parents kept arguing, he would escape facing the music for his disobedience—or at least disobedience to what one parent said but the other one contradicted—or at least disobeying one or the other while obeying one or the other—or whatever. Could anyone keep this straight, especially Rob?

Mom and Dad put on their church faces as they pulled into the parking lot. They shoved emotionally distressed Rob into his classroom, handed off shell-shocked Maggie to a doubtful nursery worker, and rushed to their Bible study group, late again.

"The topic of our lesson today is on love and unity in the body of Christ," the teacher smiled. "Isn't it wonderful how we can come from different walks of life but in our spirit and behavior have a wonderful oneness?"

"I'd settle for a little oneness in my family," Mom and Dad thought unanimously.

Anything wrong with this picture? Dad will tell you he is trying to teach the child rules and discipline. Mom will tell you she is trying to keep Dad from being too strict. Both will tell you, "If I don't do what I do, the children will grow up to become serial killers, or IRS agents, or newspaper editors who write books."

Tragically, one parent striving against the other parent is nothing new. One of the first accounts of parenthood in the Bible is about parents who were awful when it came to the business of unified guidance. Read the whole story in Genesis 25–33. It is fascinating reading of how not to raise children. One of the key passages reads,

When the boys grew up, Esau was a skillful hunter, a man of the field, while Jacob was a quiet man, living in tents. Isaac [the father] loved Esau, because he was fond of game; but Rebekah [the mother] loved Jacob. (25:27-28)

33

This may be the first significant written account of a dysfunctional family. The Bible devotes some eight and a half chapters to telling the story of how Esau and Jacob struggled most of their lives because of their parents' duplicity.

Jacob and Esau's parents were Isaac and Rebekah. Isaac was Abraham's boy, and Rebekah was a daughter of Bethuel, the Aramean, from Paddan Aram. Don't worry about saying the names right; I'm not too sure I trust people who can.

Jacob and Esau did not have a sibling rivalry going—they had a civil war going. Isaac was in Esau's corner all the way, and Rebekah was on Jacob's side right down the line.

Actually, Jacob and Esau seemed to be nice enough boys on their own. Both of them had character flaws, but overall, we probably would have liked them both if we met them at a church social. And they both grew up to be important men in the history of their parts of the world.

But the Holy Spirit inspired the writer of Genesis to record the incredible duplicity of their parents and how it contributed mightily to the boys' conflict and to interfering with God's perfect will.

Interestingly, the boys were answers to the prayers of Isaac and Rebekah. The couple reached their sixties childless, and then God sent them twins—sort of like Arnold Swartzenaegger and Danny Devito "Twins," if you remember the movie, but still twins.

Esau came out first looking like a red, furry puppy, with Jacob hanging onto his heel. Esau became a robust hunter who loved the outdoors. He was impulsive and shortsighted but had many admirable qualities—"a daddy's boy." Jacob loved staying around the tents and cooking with the girls. He was manipulative and a supplanter who was dominated by his mother—"a mama's boy."

Years ago the Smothers Brothers were a pretty fair pair of comedians who even had their own television variety show. As expected, Tom and Dick's sibling rivalry was the springboard for much of their comedy material. The younger brother Tom always said his mother loved the other brother best. "Mother gave you a puppy, but she gave me a chicken," he said. I have no idea if chickens were around when Esau and Jacob were growing up, but if they were, Rebekah surely gave Esau the chicken.

It seems as if sixty-year-old people would have known how to relate to kids, but not so. Isaac and Rebekah were not unified in their desires for their children nor in their teaching and training of them.

Father Isaac spoiled Esau rotten. The mother set about teaching Jacob how to deceive the father and exploit his brother's shortcoming. Great gifts to pass on to your children, don't you think?

The result of the parents' scheming was a life of animosities between the brothers. Understandably in human terms, the parents' actions built hatred and resentment in Esau's heart against Jacob and drove Jacob from the land. For decades, the family was alienated, and it took God's provision to redeem partially the situation. Actually, Jacob became a patriarch of the Israelites, but Esau became the father of the Ammonites. The two nations became perennial enemies.

Eventually, Jacob and Esau worked out their personal differences, but don't you imagine, if they had had a choice, they would have said, "Look, Mom and Dad, you two get together. Your double dealing is messing up even God's purpose for our lives."

Just imagine what might have happened if Isaac and Rebekah had worked as allies in the rearing of their sons? Unified guidance and discipline might not have guaranteed a unified nation of Israelites, but it would have given peace a chance.

I'm older, so I can say one of the gifts my parents gave me that I appreciate now is the gift of unified guidance and discipline. My sister and I have talked many times about our parents' solidarity in how they reared us. We thank God they were together on parenting issues. My sister and I didn't necessarily think it was all that great a deal at the time, but now that I am older and my sister is wiser, we are incredibly thankful for our parents' gift.

Regardless of what I asked one of my parents, that parent always said, "Have you asked your mother/daddy?" I hated when that happened, especially if I were trying to work one parent against the other. If I had asked my mother, and she had given me the wrong answer, and I then went to my father for a second opinion, he responded with, "Did you ask your mother?" It was truth or consequences time. If I lied, he would find out, and I would die. When I told him what Mother's answer had been, he would say, "Then, that's my answer." Never, not once in my LBA (life before adulthood), did one of my parents overturn the other. Never.

Now, they did have "talks." That was when one parent disagreed with the other or they simply needed to talk matters over before handing down a judgment.

Daddy would come nearer to letting us push the limits. I would wait until he came home and ask, "Can I go with the guys camping and fishing on the river, and everyone is going, and we will be careful, and there's never been anything go wrong—if you don't count those two kids that never came back last year or that big rattlesnake—and Joe and I told the boys you were cool, and I was sure you would let me go if I promised to show you any snakes we killed?"

"What did your mother say?"

"She said to ask you."

Conference time. I was dismissed to my room while they entered parent talk.

Daddy would then summons me to the kitchen for the verdict. "Your mother and I have decided . . . "

It was truly amazing that my father would give the verdict, without ever making it seem as if he had won or lost in the discussion. If there was a difference of opinion, he might tell me that, but he made sure I understood they were together and how they reached their decision. When I walked away, I may not have appreciated the decision, but I knew the decision was solid between my parents. There was a sense of satisfaction that my upbringing was in the hands of adults who at least acted as if they knew what they were doing. There was such comfort and security in that.

Failure to act in unity in matters of guidance and discipline is putting a time bomb in the minds of children. If you have one parent trying to get her way with the children over the wishes of the other parent, the children are fractured in their emotions and are torn by destructive choices.

For a minute, let's consider parents who are divorced and have children living at home. The temptation is great to try to convince the children that the other parent is the bad person. Some parents try to bolster their egos by contradicting the other parent's rules and guidelines. There may even be a sense of victory by making one's wishes reign while the children are in the custody of that parent. But when parents do that sort of thing, they wreak havoc on the children.

At least one parent in the divorce needs to recognize the importance of unity in parenting. Children need a good relationship with both parents. That is not possible and may not be wise all the time, but it is something the more mature, stable parent realizes and works toward.

No child should have the yoke of duplicity of parental direction forced upon him. Parents are wise to work together in giving their children direction and instruction. Duplicity of guidance and discipline puts a time bomb in the lives of children, but unified guidance and discipline plant a gift with delayed appreciation.

Time Doing "Their Thing"

"They're gonna start a soft-y-ball team at church, and they said I could play," ten-year-old Julie said, as she splattered enthusiasm all over the family room.

"You mean softball," Dad smiled.

"Yeah, that's it—softball. Dad, what is a softball team?"

Dad explained as best as anyone could explain, but he had just as soon have explained moonshots to his daughter. Her lack of understanding softball did not blunt her joy that she was going to play it.

Papa was proud, so he pulled out an old softball mitt. He was not surprised by Julie's question, "What is this for?"

When Dad, a fierce competitor, took Julie to the first practice, he discovered there were three twelve-year-olds on the team. (They were the only twelve-year-olds who wanted to play on the church's team.) But the rest were ten- and eleven-year-olds. Although most of them were like Julie—first-time players—they were placed in a league according to the oldest players.

For two weeks of practice, the girls got acquainted with the game.

Game day: Julie's team had practiced ten times. Now they faced the real thing. So, here were these rag-tag novices facing a team of which every member knew what a mitt was for and how to say the name of the game. And, oh yes, they demonstrated that they knew what a bat was for. Not a pretty sight.

Julie's parents huddled uneasily with the parents of the other team members. After two innings the parents spontaneously and unanimously chose the team's mascot—lambs, as in sacrificial lambs.

There was a rule in this league called "the mercy rule" that allowed the game to be over when every player on one team had been up to bat ten times. On this evening, that didn't take long. The rule, true to its name, put the kids to bed much earlier without making the lambs forfeit. The score: Opponents 32, Lambs 0.

Dad thought it was one of the longest nights of his life. He knew his precious daughter had learned the cruel lesson of defeat. When Julie got in the car, Dad made a valiant effort to be cheerful.

"Well, Julie, did you have a good time?"

"Oh, Daddy, it was wonderful. I loved it. I really liked being out there with all those other girls in front of all those people in those bright lights. I'm glad I'm playing soft-y-ball. Thank you for bringing me and letting me play."

She paused and then asked, "Was there a score?"

"Yes," Dad sort of laughed. "You could say that."

"What was it?"

Dad took a deep breath and broke it to her gently. "32 to nothing."

"Really! Did we win?"

Now . . . Daddy hates to lose, hates to be on a losing side, hates for his team to lose—hates it. The clear and present temptation for him was to launch into a lecture on the fine art of winning and the shame of losing. He caught himself, realizing this was Julie's time, and she had a right to enjoy it at her level of participation. He realized she would learn the lesson of victory and defeat soon enough.

"Great, Honey. I'm glad you enjoyed it. It was fun being
with all those friends and having a good time."
"When do we play again, Daddy?"

Being with your child is important, but being with her at her
level of participation and understanding is every bit as
important. I learned that lesson too late, and it cost me a hunting
partner.

When we moved to Louisiana, I learned that deer hunting
for multitudes is as important, as, well . . . I can't think of anything else that is as important to those folks, except maybe
Louisiana State University athletics or else fishing. You get the
idea.

Finding or arranging a place to hunt is as difficult as . . . getting tickets to an LSU football game. But one day, in an obscure
page of the daily newspaper, there appeared a notice that a
wildlife area near our home would allow a limited number of
hunters to try their skills at harvesting a deer. I applied for a
"youth permit" for my ten-year-old son, and our names were
drawn for one of the permits. Now we could join the
conversation at all the social gatherings.

I was thrilled; Ron wasn't particularly. I scouted the area and
was set for the day of the hunt. I dragged Ron out of bed at 3
A.M. and headed to the wildlife area. He slept all the way there
and only reluctantly followed me out of the car when we arrived
for the hunt. Explaining why we were there before daylight was
not easy.

We climbed the tree I had located and took our stand. So did
the fire ants. Ron simply could not understand why I demanded
stillness and silence from him when fire ants were having a feast
on his legs. Telling him they were biting me too was no solace.
The morning pretty well went that way.

About eight o'clock another father and his two sons, one about ten and one about seven, came trudging by our stand. The father was obviously disgusted. "I can't believe these boys. They wouldn't stay in the stand. They said they had rather be home watching cartoons than out here hunting. Can you believe that? I'm tired of arguing with them. We're going home." The two embarrassed brothers tucked their heads but kept walking.

Ron and I sat there in silence for a while, then he asked, "Dad, what time is it?"

"8:15."

Long pause . . . "We could get home for the last of the cartoons if we left right now."

Any time after that I mentioned going deer hunt, Ron jumped up and ran away as fast as his fire-ant-scarred legs would carry him. Never went with me again. Never. I was spending time with my son, doing something he said he had wanted to do, but I was doing it at my level of interest.

Children want their parents to be with them, but they don't get all excited about being with their parents. They spend too much of their lives just being with their parents—usually waiting for them. They want their parents to be with them some of the time.

Once when I visited a really nice house, I was shocked when I walked into the usually sparkling kitchen. There beside a cooking island stood a seven-year-old girl and her mother, both absolutely covered with flour. Every inch of their aprons, every square inch of their faces, and even their hair was flour-saturated. If it hadn't been July in Louisiana, one could have thought a freak snowstorm had swept through the place. The daughter was obviously happy, and the mother managed a smile.

"This is her time to make a cake. I'm helping her make the cake."

"Maybe you should think about letting her help you."

"Nope. On her day I help her." The mother looked around at the mound of mess and said, "Kitchens clean up."

Kitchens do clean up, but the bond of a daughter having her mother help her bake doesn't go away. The older the daughter gets, the more appreciated those mother-daughter times become. My guess is that every time that daughter bakes a cake for her husband or someone else nowadays, she feels the gift of her mother's presence.

Have you ever thought about the irony of parents going to all the trouble and involvement to bring children into the world and then hating to invest time with them? Why would we bring children into the world if we did not want to enjoy them? What right do we have to birth children if we are not going to nurture them?

Children do not ask to come into the world; they have absolutely no say about it—not when, where, nor to whom. We bring them in, usually kicking and screaming. We asked for them. Sometimes we are like my daughter, who used to bring home every imaginable kind of animal and then expect me to care for it. We bring children into the world because it seems like such a neat idea, but then we seem to expect them to raise themselves. We want to spend our time on more important things, or at least things more important to us.

One day a pastor was giving me a tour of his congregation's new education building. It was a beauty, especially for the small church in a mission setting. We were walking through the children's area, and over on a corkboard were posted pictures the children had drawn of their families. Finding the picture of the pastor's child was a no-brainer; the pastor had twelve children. The little girl had drawn carefully and with surprising detail her mother and each of her brothers and sisters. Beside the mother stood a large question mark. The child simply did not have enough recollection of her father to draw anything beyond a question mark. We walked through the rest of the building, but the dad didn't say a word. The building had lost a considerable amount of its luster.

How many children have question marks instead of fathers or mothers? You can say what you want about so-called quality time, but there is nothing you can give your children that is more important to them than time—and lots of it. Give your children a gift they will appreciate when they are older. Find an activity they enjoy, and then spend time doing it with them, at their level of enjoyment.

Last year I interviewed a group of ladies who gather weekly to quilt. I asked each lady, all of them retired and several living alone, how they learned to quilt. Everyone of them said they learned to quilt "watching my mother and doing whatever part of quilting I could do." Each of the mothers had made time to patiently teach her daughter to quilt and let her participate at her level of interest—a small gift, maybe some would say a tiny gift.

Each of the quilters said she had laid aside quilting for many years but started again. The main reason these ladies quilt now—sixty, seventy, even eighty years later—is because when they quilt, they feel close to their mothers. One lady, in her late seventies, could not finish her explanation of how close she felt to her mother as she quilted. The emotions of those memories caused her to stop talking and dab her eyes with a tissue.

I doubt there was any way this dear lady's mother could have known what a wonderful gift she was giving her daughter on those days she took that little bit of extra time to be with her daughter, at her level of interest. And I doubt if the mother could have known how long that gift would last or that it would take a few years to be fully appreciated. If the mother had known how important it was, she might have tried to make too big a deal over it!

If you want to read not a success story but a tragic story of parenting, read 2 Samuel 13-19:8. King David did a lot of things really well, but apparently spending time with his kids was not one of them. He and his son both paid the price. David's words are truly the saddest of tongue or pen: "O my son Absalom! . . . Would I had died instead of you, O Absalom, my son, my son" (18:33). I imagine if David had it to do over again, he would have given Absalom the gift of time.

A Home and Welcome for All

"Dad, could we take several friends to a really nice restaurant for my birthday?"

Time was nearing for Stephanie's 13th birthday. We had begun talking about possible appropriate celebrations.

I pondered the matter, primarily the expense, and said, "Okay, we can do that. You can bring 3 friends because that number will fit easily in one car."

A few days later: "Dad, could we maybe take a few more friends?"

"How many more?"

"Maybe 5 more."

"Well, I guess I could borrow a van and do that, but we can't go to as nice a place."

A few days later: "Daddy, can I have a few more friends?"

"Like how many?"

"Like, maybe, 10 more."

Long pause . . . "Okay. I guess I can get someone to drive their van and follow me in the borrowed van. But we will have to go to a pizza place."

Two days before the party: "Daddy, I think we may have a few more people coming to the party."

"How many more?"

"Maybe 10."

"10? Are you talking 25?"

"Yes."

"Well, we are going to have to have it at home, and I will order the pizza. I'll get a couple of sets of parents to come help me."

"Thanks, Dad."

The night of the party the number grew to somewhere between 45 and 50—they never stood still long enough for me to count them all. They came through the kitchen and moved out onto the backyard—the backyard with the grass I had slaved over for several years, nursing it back from child-inflicted abuse.

The kids were a great group. They just sort of shuffled around from little group to little group. They moved around the backyard and front yard like wildebeests. The amount of pizza they consumed could have been entered into the Guinness Book of Records, if we had been just a little more careful with our record keeping.

The next morning I wandered into the backyard that had been covered with lush turf, assessing the damage. The dirt was as barren as the concrete driveway. My grass had vanished under 100 shuffling feet.

Later my daughter came out of the house. She didn't notice the barren yard. She just gave me a hug and said, "Thanks, Dad. It was a great party, and the kids thought the house and yard are cool. They want to come back."

I swallowed hard.

When my children were living at home, I wanted them to enjoy being at their home as much as they enjoyed being anywhere. Of course, my desire was a little idealistic. At times they would have preferred to be anywhere else on the planet rather than home. But then, I understand. There were times when I would have preferred to be anywhere else—especially when the children were home! Maybe I should say that the ideal is to make home a place your children do not mind being most of the time.

When my oldest son reached the time in life that he could go to his friends' homes, I tried to notice the kinds of homes he was always ready to visit. Some of the homes were large and loaded with gadgets and games children love, with swimming pools in the backyards. Some of the homes were small and crowded with very few whistles and bells. I was amused to notice that he did not always find his way to the large, loaded homes. He more frequently found his way to a smaller, very modest house. That puzzled me.

One day I drove to the small house to retrieve him. I knocked on the back door—I still do not know why we have front doors in the South, except for the entrance of salespersons and preachers—and was greeted by the father of the house. As I stepped into the small "family area," I almost had to step over furniture just to get into the room. But I could feel the family warmth. There was just something about the spirit of the house that said, "You are welcome in this place." Although the house was small, the mother walked back to the boy's room and knocked on the door. "Ron, your father is here," she said kindly. Ron emerged with his friend and said, "Let me put the stuff up." That was a shock within itself—my son putting up "stuff."

Driving home, I asked Ron, "Why do you like to go over there?" He had a ready answer: "Daddy, Mr. and Mrs. Guidry (not their real name) are the nicest people. They are friendly to you, and they just talk to you about stuff you are doing. They let us go in Jim's room and play his guitar as long as we don't get too loud. She fixes snacks and stuff. You just really feel good there."

I thought about it, and as close as I could figure, Ron liked going there because they treated him like an adult, or as adult as a ten-year-old could be treated. I got some pretty good ideas about what kind of atmosphere Ron needed to feel welcome in his own home.

Early on, my son was into magic, not tricks you can do on the kitchen table or in the den, but illusions such as making things, people, and animals disappear. He frequently turned our backyard into stages for elaborate illusions. The illusions were roughly hewed, but they were grand. One of his favorite, oft-repeated acts was making our Pomeranian puppy, Foxy, disappear. He used pieces of scrap plywood and wire milk carton cases and old sheets and whatever else to build his props. Ron put poor Foxy through the throws of "disappearing" until Foxy ran and hid in the shrubs when he saw the stage construction begin.

Once the stage was set and the props worked out, Ron would go through the neighborhood gathering an audience. His sister was his "beautiful assistant," and I was the dispenser of cokes and popcorn. I'm not sure what the neighborhood folks thought about all of this, but they kept coming back, or at least most of them did.

There were tools that disappeared with the acts. Ron and I could never figure out how to make the mess disappear after the shows. And more than once he used some really nice lumber I was saving for a special project. But his building stages and props in the backyard was a hundred times better than not being able to find him.

Later Ron took up drums. I don't need to tell you what that was like. I looked forward to the day his interest changed. It did: he added an electric guitar. Fortunately, he could not play the drums and guitar at the same time. Unfortunately, friends came over to do that. Honestly, I loved it when he was into all that stuff.

When my children got older and started "going out," I still tried to make their home visitor-friendly. I'm not sure kids date in the sense previous generations dated. Groups of them just sort of get together and "hang out." It is amazing any of them ever get married nowadays. They usually "stage" for the evening somewhere and then go off to do whatever comes to mind.

Stephanie enjoyed not just "hanging out," but hanging out with a lot of friends. That birthday pizza party must have really impressed her psyche. Our house became her friends' staging area. Every Friday and Saturday night—every one of them—for thirty minutes before the appointed time of departure, ten to twenty teenagers would be in the family room.

This gathering ran up the soft drink and snack bill, but I loved the kids being around. I enjoyed getting to know them because they were bright, funny, energetic, good-looking, and aware. Their coming to our house gave me an opportunity to know my daughter's friends—who she was "hanging out" with. Some of them I questioned her about; some I bragged on. I could listen and know what they were up to. By knowing my daughter's friends, I also knew which parents I could check with when my children would tell me something I felt just a little suspicious of.

As parents we are entrusted with caring not only for our children, but for others of God's children. A major part of that responsibility is creating a home that loves God and one another, that extends a warm welcome to all.

When I graduated from high school, we lived in Temple, Oklahoma, a place in the rich wheat lands of the Great Plains. Our economy revolved around farming wheat, including the grand time of year, the harvest. Several people in our area "followed the harvest." They loaded wheat harvesting combines on the backs of trucks, and as the edge of the harvest moved north, so did those harvesting crews.

I had the opportunity to join one of those crews, and my parents reluctantly agreed to let me go. We followed the harvest from Texas to North Dakota, leaving home in mid-June and not returning until late August. I was seldom able to talk with my parents by phone, and you can imagine how seldom I wrote letters.

Now I understand how they must have worried. Working in the harvest was hard, fatiguing, often remote, and dangerous—especially for a kid who had just graduated from high school and had never been away from home longer than a week. The wheels of the combines were just as good at cutting off human digits and limbs as wheat, and the trucks top-heavy with combines or loaded with wheat flipped easily.

We finally got back home early one morning as darkness still hid most of our little town. Mother and Daddy and my little sister, Judy, got up to greet me. I then went to sleep. My bed never felt so wonderful!

The next morning my dad told me, "Come on, Son."

I followed him to the car. He drove into the country to the home of the family with whom I went on harvest. The man was working on a combine sitting in the edge of a field. My dad walked across the lot to him. My dad, with genuine emotion, stuck out his hand to the farmer's. As they shook hands, my dad said simply, "Thanks for taking care of my boy."

That was all he said, but suddenly I realized that farmer was one of the most important men in my dad's life because he looked after me that summer. We turned around, walked back to the car, and rode silently back to town.

I have thought about Joseph in the Bible and how he cared for God's son. In a sense, he was a surrogate parent. He protected

Jesus through all the threats and dangers of Jesus' first years and must have made the family a place of great love. I just imagine that when Joseph died and went to heaven, God stopped whatever He was doing and walked to the gates of heaven to greet Joseph. I think God gave Joseph a big hug and said, "Thanks for taking care of my boy."

One day, as a Christian parent, you will enter those heavenly gates. When you do, I hope God walks over to you, gives you a hug, and says, "Thanks for taking care of my child."

Responsibility for
Actions and Consequences

"Afternoon, Mrs. Adams."

"Afternoon, Mr. Boone."

Mrs. Adams' turn in line had come, as parents in cars waited to pick up their children at the elementary school.

Mr. Boone walked to the car and opened the door for the book-ladened third grader.

"You have a good evening, now, Belinda," the good-natured principal said smiling, "and mind your mother."

The little girl looked up from the car's back seat to give Mr. Boone a quick glance of aggravation. The mother did not smile, but waited for the door to close and then quickly drove off.

As the car pulled around the circle in front of the school, the wise, battle-worn principal said to me, "Well, I'm glad to see her coming to school for some reason other than saving her daughter and straightening us out. Every time her daughter gets into any kind of difficulty or trouble, the mother rushes to the school to 'straighten things out.' She is the most straightening woman I've ever seen! I guess she will be saving Belinda for the rest of her life. God help the man that ends up marrying that little girl. Her mother will be right in the middle of every argument, making sure her daughter gets her way. I wonder if that mother understands the terrible effect that saving her daughter from any pain or hassle is having on the girl. Belinda may like it now, but

*when she gets older, she's going to understand that, mother or
not, improper behavior eventually has very unpleasant consequences. She is going to resent her mother for giving her all
this now."*

"You have the right to choose your actions; you do not have
the right to choose the consequences of those actions."

I heard a preacher say those words more than a quarter of a century ago. He might be surprised to know something he said
made such an impression on a listener that it would be quoted
in a book twenty-five-plus years later. The wisdom of his words
struck my heart and made an indelible impression on my mind.

Parents spend a tremendous amount of time trying to teach
their children that actions have consequences. We teach our
small children: stick your hand in a fire, and it will get burned;
jump out of a moving car, and you will get hurt; play in the traffic, and you are liable to get hit by an automobile. Until our
children understand these and thousands of other important
actions/consequences, we try to keep them from the actions and
therefore the consequences. We try to keep them away from fires,
grab them when they try to jump out of a car, and keep them
from playing in the street. These are the actions of any sane,
caring parent.

But some parents never let their children grow beyond this
stage. They are always trying to save their children from the negative consequences of their actions. The parents do not allow the
distance that is necessary for the children to learn from their mis-
takes. It takes this kind of learning for the children to grow up
mentally mature, develop self-esteem, and become responsible
adults.

Some counselors say such overprotecting grows from guilt.
Others believe it grows from insecurity. Others insist it grows

from the desire to control. Whatever its source, overprotecting is not healthy.

No emotionally balanced parent wants to see her children suffer, but a wise parent gently disengages from overinvolvement in a child's life to let the child understand that actions have consequences. We hope and pray our children learn not to play in traffic, but we cannot follow them around for the rest of their lives reminding them to be careful crossing the street. Sooner or later they must become responsible for themselves in street crossing.

In addition, wise parents work with their children as the children work through problems and difficulties. If a child learns how to deal with problems the life of a 10-year-old presents, he is more likely to be able to handle the problems an 11-year-old faces. If a child regularly forgets to take his homework to school, rather than the parent always rushing to school with it, the child should learn by facing the consequences of forgetting the homework. If he learns that lesson, he is far more likely to remember to take his briefcase to the office when he is 57!

I've tried to live by this, but in all honesty, it's not easy. While struggling through her freshman year in high school, my daughter burst into the house one afternoon, slammed her books on the kitchen counter, and cried, "She is crazy. She is a nut. She makes me so mad, I . . . "

Being a caring, feeling parent, I sensed something might have gone wrong that day. "What's wrong, baby?" I said as sympathetically as I could muster.

For the next five minutes my daughter ranted and raved about a particular teacher. Every third sentence was, "She's crazy," or "I hate her."

I reminded Stephanie that she was not to say such rude things about another person. But here's the kicker: I agreed with her. I knew the lady, and while she was not certifiably crazy, she was a ball of neuroticism. Honestly, I didn't much care to be around her, either, especially since she had harassed my darling baby. I listened, frantically tried to figure out how I was going to respond, and prayed. Parents can do at least three things at once while under offspring duress.

After Stephanie spewed off enough steam to settle down to something resembling a reasonable state of mind, I said: "Darling (parents call their kids these kinds of names at times like this), I know exactly what you are saying. I know she really did some things that do not seem logical to you and, quite frankly, to me. But as much as you do not want to hear it, the world is full of people like her, and you might as well learn to deal with them now. You will run into them at every point in life. I tell you what. Let's think about how you can deal with this. And, I promise you, if she keeps going like this, and you can't deal with it, I'll go to the school and talk to the principal."

To my amazement, that provided enough encouragement to my daughter. She took a deep breath, and said, "Okay. If you promise." I promised.

The year was not an easy one in that class. But to my daughter's credit, she worked through it and in the process began to learn how to deal with difficult people in positions of authority. Thankfully, I didn't have to go to the school to talk to the principal about it! Principals always make me nervous. As one guy said, "I love school; it's the principal of the thing that bothers me."

There is a great deal of talk and writing about "enabling" people to behave badly without letting them experience the full consequences of their actions. This realization is an important part of helping addicts to recover from their addiction. For instance, an alcoholic man often has an enabling wife. She covers for him and justifies and rationalizes his actions to others, especially his family, friends, and employer. As long as the wife continues her enabling behavior, the alcoholic is less likely to pay the price for recovery. She must struggle as strongly to stop enabling as he does to stop drinking.

Parents often become enablers for their children's inappropriate behavior. Such enabling keeps the children from growing up and becoming increasingly responsible.

Some folks call it tough love, but there comes a time when parents have to step back and let their children experience the consequences of inappropriate behavior. This is incredibly painful for the parents but necessary for the children's maturity.

On the other hand, some parents have a difficult time letting their children experience the positive consequences of positive behavior. These parents seem never satisfied with their child's behavior and accomplishments. There are probably a lot of motivations for such behavior, but whatever the motivation, the behavior is damaging to the child's self-image.

My parents' greatest fears concerning their children were two: (1) we would embarrass them with unchristian or inappropriate public behavior, or (2) we might in some far-fetched way become conceited. The result of their second fear was that they seldom complimented us or "bragged" on what we did.

When I was a freshman in high school, my dad accepted a pastorate in another village. Moving at that age was traumatic, and we three kids suffered. But at the end of the school year, miracle of miracles, I was elected class favorite. Not a particularly stellar accomplishment in a class of twenty-eight, but for me, it was unbelievable. I was stunned and could hardly wait to get home to tell my parents. I rushed into the house and blurted the news to Mother, who suffered painful insecurities. She said simply, "It's because you are new. We'll see if you get it next year."

To this day I feel bad when I think about that, and I have seldom looked at the "Freshman Favorites" page in the yearbook. She meant well, but it probably would have been better if she had let me experience the positive results of the honor. Besides, it didn't work. I still grew to be conceited!

I have tried to be different with my children. When they receive any kind of honor or achieve some accomplishment, large or small, we have celebrations. When the children were small, we would do a little something that was special to them. As they got older, we went to a special place to eat. Now I take them out to eat and buy some little gift. We don't make a really big deal of it, but we recognize it. These celebrations do not add fuel to their conceit, but they do marvels for their confidence. They help my children to take their accomplishments and honors in stride.

We do get wrapped up in our children, often seeing them as little more than extensions of our successes and failures.

A couple of summers ago, I was walking the street in downtown Creede, Colorado, a tiny mining town surrounded by summer homes and cabins. I ran into a great friend. For years I have enjoyed visiting with this older friend as we both escape there to our cabins.

We sat on a bench in front of one of the stores and caught up with each other's year. Then he paused, as though there was something more important he needed to talk about. I asked him, "How is it going?" He responded, "Not too well."

Then he poured out his broken heart of a son who had left his position as a university professor to "drop out" and play in a bar band. He also had left his wife and was living with a woman who had ridden with a motorcycle gang. The blow to this wonderful father, an outstanding Christian and a greatly admired and respected man in his city, was unbelievable. The pain dripped from his face.

I asked, "How old is your son?" believing he would say he was in his early 30s.

He answered, "47."

"I think he is old enough to know what he is doing," I reminded him. "You know you are not responsible for him."

"I know, but I feel like I am."

I suddenly changed the discussion to the man's daughter, whom I knew to be a well-known author and speaker. His face lit up as he talked about her, her recent honors, her books, her accomplishments.

"I'll tell you what," I said to him, "if you will not take credit for your daughter, I will not blame you for your son."

A light went on, and he said, "I see what you mean."

We come to a point when we should let our children be responsible for themselves. We can free them by degrees, allowing them to adjust and grow, so that we do not simply drop them out of the nest one day when they least expect it.

I have often thought of the parable of the Prodigal Son. There are several points we can make from the story, but the thing that strikes me is that a major part of the father's love was shown as he let the prodigal go his way and do his own thing. The father obviously knew the son was not mature enough to handle a significant amount of wealth, and I guess he also knew the only way the son would learn his lesson was to let him suffer the consequences of his actions. There was great risk in what the father did—the son might have lost his life in the kinds of places he lived. But the father knew the risk was necessary.

How long was the time from when the son left the father's house until he returned? We do not know, but it must have been a substantial amount of time. The son could not fully appreciate what the father was doing when he let him go. There may have been times the son was angry because his father did not come looking for him nor save him from the pig pens. The son probably did not see his father's letting him suffer the consequences of his actions as a cherished gift. But later the errant son certainly appreciated his father's gift. Also notice, when the son came home, the father let him experience the positive consequences of his positive actions. The celebration was significant.

A Positive Attitude and Affirmation

When my children were twelve and six, we decided to turn a business trip of mine into a marvelous cross-country train excursion. When I told my friends about our decision, some of them warned me that the train experience might not be entirely pleasant, due to conditions on passenger trains they had experienced.

As we waited with anticipation for the train—which was three hours late—I pulled everyone together and said, "Look, I don't know what is ahead on this trip, but I can tell you one thing. It is not what happens to us as much as how we react."

I was on a roll, like a football coach before a big game.

"We are going to look at everything on this trip as a happening. Everything that happens is going to be part of our overall memory of this experience. Let's just take whatever comes and see the humor in it and realize that for the rest of our lives, we will remember this. Let's look at it with a positive attitude and not get upset about anything that happens. Let's not let anything that happens ruin this tremendous experience."

It was one of my best presentations ever, and they fell for it! It was a good thing because we had many challenges that could have been disastrous. Whatever happened, we laughed at it and realized that later it would be part of our memories. We knew disasters are the things we talk about most and laugh at the hardest.

Our train compartment was a wreck. Every time we ran water into the lavatory, the water poured onto the floor. The commode worked only occasionally. The train was eight hours late getting to Chicago, etc., etc., etc. All this happened on the first leg of the trip, so you get the idea. While these matters were inconveniences, they did not ruin our trip. We still look back at those ten days as a wonderful, educational, inspiring, fun time.

We made the decision to be positive regardless—and there were ample "regardlesses." We could not keep the trying circumstances from intruding into our trip, but we could determine the spirit with which we met them. If my kids learned anything at all about being positive on that trip, that alone was worth the price of the train tickets.

I learned the power of a positive attitude from someone who lived it: my mother. She lived in a disciplined positive frame of mind until her death.

"I'm so glad you are here. It's so good to see you. You always make me feel so much better when you come to see me." That's how my mother greeted me every time I visited her in the nursing home in which she lived for the last two years of her life. That may not seem like a big deal, but when I heard other residents greet their visitors, I realized anew what a great gift Mother's positive greeting was. I heard other residents greet their guests with, "Well, it is about time you came to see me." "It's been so long since you were here, I thought maybe you were dead." "Where have you been? I get so tired of sitting here waiting for someone to come see me." "Where have you been?"

Mother's positive spirit went beyond greetings. Any time anyone asked her how she was doing, inevitably her answer was: "Great. I feel fine. I don't have a pain. I don't hurt anywhere." I often teased her by saying those words along with her, and a big smile would break across her face. If she told me she was hurting in some way, I took it with utmost seriousness.

The difference between Mother's positive greetings, even when her mind was severely damaged by dementia, and the negative greetings she could have given was not due to circumstances. Some folks visited their nursing homebound loved ones every day, and there were some times I wasn't able to visit mother for periods as long as two weeks. My mother's positive response was a continuation of a lifestyle she worked tirelessly to develop. She learned to major on the positive. She spoke the positive. She imparted the positive. It was one of the greatest gifts to anyone who knew her.

It wasn't that she didn't have ample reasons to be negative. She had a life that was filled with trials. She suffered rheumatic fever when she was six and then had Saint Vitus' Dance, a terribly debilitating neurological ailment, part of which was a kind of mental illness. Her mother's love, coupled with her own determination forged by her faith in God, pulled her back to health, and she began to understand the power of a positive attitude and faith. Later in life she experienced several major surgeries and the trials of being a sensitive woman married to a strong-willed and often critical preacher. She felt her emotions deeply. But she learned to look for the positives of every situation. She chose to be positive and helped her children to do the same.

The older I grow, the more I appreciate the marvelous gift of a positive attitude Mother gave me. My friends say Mother did a great job of imparting her positive attitude to me. They will tell you I do not like negativism in any shape, form, or fashion.

A positive attitude is one of life's greatest converters. It can convert any situation into something with positive memories and results. You can give your children this wonderful converter if you impart the gift of a positive attitude.

A friend of mine took his daughter backpacking in a wilderness area of Colorado. She was graduating from college and would start her life as an independent, grown woman within months. The backpacking expedition was to be a special time with her father, with whom she was great friends.

The bane of backpacking is rain. When the rain becomes severe, there is little to do but set up the tent and sit in it. There is nothing more confining and boring than staring at the inside of a backpacker's tiny tent. During the father-daughter outing the rain came, and came, and came. The father remained his positive self, and his daughter was caught up in the spirit. They made the best of sitting in a tiny tent, talking about significant experiences of the past and dreaming about the future. The experience wasn't what they planned or even wanted, but the experience will be part of their special relationship. They had no control over the rain, but they did have control over how they responded. They met it head-on with a positive attitude.

In math, two negatives may equal a positive, but in life, two negatives do not add to one another; they multiply both negatives into a mass of negativism. However, a positive reaction to a negative situation can cancel the debilitating effect of the negative. So, you can imagine what happens when positive meets positive!

If you want to give your children a great gift, give them an example of a positive, transforming attitude. I speak from firsthand experience when I tell you how this approach to life can affect your offspring, who will grow to appreciate it more the older they get.

When my mother was 72 years of age, I found myself a single parent with primary, residential custody of a 9-year-old daughter and a 15-year-old son. Mother came from Kansas to Louisiana to help me get on my feet in this challenging situation. One month later we learned my father had a fatal brain tumor. In 4 months my mother lost her husband of 50 years and faced other severe changes.

We traveled back to Wichita to sell the two-bedroom house that had been their home for ten years—the only house they ever owned. We sold all of their earthly belongings. Mother pocketed less than $2,000 for her possessions, and less than $5,000 for the house. My sister and I were in continuous tears as we watched people carry off the beds we slept in as children, the sofa mother had been so proud of the day the furniture people delivered it, the washer and dryer she had paid on for years. . . . But Mother, while deeply saddened, kept saying: "You kids stop acting that way. They are just things; they are just things. It's family and faith that matter, and we still have that. Those are just things."

Mother moved in with the kids and me and accepted the challenge of helping me care for two children. At her funeral my daughter, then twenty-one, insisted on delivering her Gran's eulogy. In that eulogy she paid homage to the indomitable positive attitude her Gran exhibited and its impact upon her. It may be a few years before Stephanie masters her Gran's art of positive response to all circumstances, but she knows where she is headed. And the older she gets, the more she appreciates that marvelous gift her grandmother gave her.

And now, a word about affirmation.

One of the most overlooked ministries of Christians is that of affirming. You probably don't think about affirmation as a ministry. References to it are found throughout the New Testament, such as in 1 Corinthians 1:6, ". . . the testimony of Christ has been strengthened among you." In your family life, be alert to ways you can affirm your children. Affirm who they are as well as what they do.

A friend of mine shared a great suggestion for parents who believe they have lost the opportunity to help their children feel affirmed. A preacher-father told me, "I was so busy building a church when my boys were growing up, I simply did not spend enough time with them to help them feel that I cherished them. They were all grown up when I realized my failure. But a wise man told me, 'Preacher, what you need to do is get in the letter-writing business. The next time one of your boys has a special day, like a birthday, write him a letter. Tell him how much you appreciate him. Try to think of something he did that revealed solid character, and tell him about it.' "

"Well, I could hardly wait for one of the boys to have a special day. I wrote my second-oldest son a letter on Father's Day and just tried to let him know that I cherish him for being my son. The next time I saw him, he gave me a big hug and thanked me for the letter. 'Dad, it was like someone filled a big hole that had been in my heart.' "

Somewhere I read about an experiment that illustrates how we as parents impact our children. A father of three small children learned he had a terminal illness and surely would be dead in a matter of a few months. His wife saw her husband go to his desk early every day and write continuously and thoughtfully on a legal pad. Periodically, he would tear the filled pages from the pad and place them in an envelope, seal the envelope, and write something on the envelopes. Finally, he called his wife to the desk and explained: "In a few months I will be gone. I will not be here for my children's birthdays, graduations, marriages . . . But I want them to know on those important days that I love them. I have written each of them a special letter for those days. I've written the name of the child for whom I wrote the letter and the occasion for which I have written it. I want them to have my presence with them in a special way and to know that my absence is not because of a lack of love."

What a magnificent gesture! But you know, we write letters to our children every day. We write across their hearts and memories in indelible ink. We write messages that will be with them every day of their lives. The only question is, what will we write?

Love for the Church

The snow was deep on a dark Kansas evening. Attendance at Wednesday prayer service was sparse. Our regular pianist and the back-ups were at home, keeping toasty warm.

"Well, I don't see any of our pianists. Do any of you play the piano?" I asked in half-jest of the handful of familiar people.

Joyce raised her hand and then moved to the piano. I was shocked.

Joyce was a shy young-adult lady who joined our chuch about a year earlier. She was regular in attendance, as her presence that evening demonstrated, but she said very little in group discussions or any other time.

She sat down at the piano and played great! Afterward I asked how she came to play the piano so well. She told me that her family attended a small church when she and her four sisters and a brother were growing up.

"One Sunday morning, there was no pianist to play for worship. We had a visiting family who did not come back, and my dad was certain it was because we had such bad music that Sunday. The next week he went out and bought a $50 piano and took us six kids to a piano teacher and started us all taking piano. It was a real financial sacrifice for him.

"Before the lessons began, he set us all down and told us, 'I want you kids to learn well and learn fast. The next time someone wants to know if there is a piano player in the church, you had better volunteer. I don't ever want to hear *of any church meeting needing a piano player with you in the congregation and you not playing. That's why you are getting the lessons. Any questions?' "*

Joyce smiled and added, "He didn't say we have to volunteer on our own. Only play if someone asks for a pianist!"

What a gift! As far as Joyce knew, the six children, now grown, were all actively committed to their churches, and each one volunteered to play the piano, at least when no other pianist was present! Such love and involvement by adult children of church folks are not always the case.

The sadness of his expression and voice made me want to give him a hug of comfort. He had been going on and on about his two grown children. He beamed as he told me about their vocational accomplishments, mates, and children. He was proud of his children and proud of the job he and his wife did raising them. Then his eyes dropped in thought, and he said, "But they don't go to church like I want them to—like they should." What he meant was, they do not go at all. "I wish it were different; I wish I had done something differently."

There is no perfect, sure-fire vaccination against this tragedy. There is no guarantee against the children of even the finest, most church-active parents forsaking their churches, and even their faith. That can happen to anyone's children. People constantly quote, "Raise up a child in the way he should go, and when he is old, he will not depart from it." But that is a statement of the ideal, not an absolute promise. If it were an absolute promise, it would work every time. A lot of folks will say, "Well, to us, they may look like they raised that child right, but we don't know what they really taught him." Rather than looking for excuses of why the promise did not work, let's acknowledge that any time human will is involved, there is the chance a person will not choose the right and best way.

But parents can give their children a wonderful gift the children will appreciate when they are older. I have watched families in their interaction with the church for half a century, and it seems some parents impart an attitude that helps their children develop an ongoing, meaningful, involved relationship with their church.

Some parents give their children the wonderful gift of always speaking well of the church and its staff. The children see their parents' priority of participating in the activities of the church, and they hear their parents talk joyfully of supporting the church financially. The old cliché is true: "Religion is caught more than taught."

Most parents want their children to be just a little more active in church than they are, their children's faith to be a little stronger than theirs is, and their moral behavior to be better than theirs was growing up. But many of these same parents maintain minimal commitment to the church. Conversation about the church around the house is, "Well, they can talk about tithing all they want, and that's fine for people who can afford it, but there is no way we are going to give 10 percent to the church. They waste too much money, anyway." These parents put their money where their mouth is and give their children a dollar or less to put into their offering envelopes. When revivals or other special activities roll around, the parents may go and take their children—on those times when absolutely nothing else interferes. But if anything else—anything—comes up, the church activity is left to fend for itself.

Through all of this, the kids understand clearly what their parents are saying: Church, and therefore its teachings, is a take-it-or-leave-it proposition. The children come to understand that religion and church are optional. It ranks pretty well at the bottom of obligations. They come to the conclusion that the church represents faith and moral behavior, so if church is an option in a cafeteria-style world, then what it stands for and teaches is optional. Church is just another nice organization, but it is not necessary. It is little wonder that when these children get older, church is often discarded as the offspring discover the importance of working, recreating, or just plain sleeping late.

I have not undertaken any kind of scientific study, but it seems when parents demonstrate minimal commitment to the church, their children give even less commitment than did their parents. Usually and tragically, the children drift further away from the church and Christ.

When I was a youth minister, a family in the church had two sons in our group. The older was an outstanding young man. He found great fulfillment in his relationship with Christ, and his participation in our youth activities became more and more important to him. His parents did not understand his participation. They were fine, outstanding community leaders, but only "Sunday morning members." One Saturday morning the older son was getting ready to participate in a work day at the mission building. He was skipping an activity of an important club to do mission work. His mother was less than pleased and said sternly, "Everything that goes on in the world does not go on at _____" —and she gave the address of the church.

But parents with minimal commitment to the activities of the church are not the only ones who may be discouraging their kids in matters of faith. Some parents who have their families at every meeting announced in the church newsletter make a major mistake in demonstrating a poor attitude toward church. These parents serve on committees and help with endless tasks, but they constantly vent frustration and discontentment and even anger about the church in the presence of their children. They criticize the pastor and church leadership. They rewrite the verse that says "Be thankful for everything" to "Gripe and complain about everything." These parents would be wise to realize what they are teaching their children with this kind of behavior. They would also be wise to understand that this kind of behavior likely will bring disappointment with their children's relationship to the church down the road.

There is something extraordinarily difficult about passing on a mild case of religion: mild cases usually prove to be vaccinations that prevent a strong case of the real thing. One thing for sure, I've never heard of anyone willing to die for a mild case of religion! It is extremely difficult to pass on a positive attitude toward the church when the atmosphere around the house is strongly negative toward the church.

There has never been a better statement about parental responsibility concerning religion than the following passage found in Deuteronomy. It contains one of the greatest gifts you can give your children—the example of a vibrant, committed faith.

> Hear, O Israel: The Lord is our God, the Lord alone. You shall love the Lord your God with all your heart, and with all your soul, and with all your might. Keep these words that I am commanding you today in your heart. Recite them to your children and talk about them when you are at home and when you are away, when you lie down and when you rise. Bind them as a sign on your hand, fix them as an emblem on your forehead, and write them on the doorposts of your house and on your gates.
>
> When the Lord your God has brought you into the land that he swore to your ancestors, to Abraham, to Isaac, and to Jacob, to give you—a land with fine, large cities that you did not build, houses filled with all sorts of goods that you did not fill, hewn cisterns that you did not hew, vineyards and olive groves that you did not plant—and when you have eaten your

fill, take care that you do not forget the Lord, who brought you out of the land of Egypt, out of the house of slavery. The Lord your God you shall fear; him you shall serve, and by his name alone you shall swear. . . .

When your children ask you in time to come, "What is the meaning of the decrees and the statutes and the ordinances that the Lord our God has commanded you?" then you shall say to your children, "We were Pharaoh's slaves in Egypt, but the Lord brought us out of Egypt with a mighty hand. . . . Then the Lord commanded us to observe all these statutes, to fear the Lord our God, for our lasting good, so as to keep us alive, as is now the case." (6:4-13, 20, 21, 24)

My dad was a minister and loved the church. This does not mean the churches he served as pastor were always lovable. I can tell you, to me, they were not. Two of them fired my father. I believe I could prove in any court of law in the land that he was innocent of the charges they leveled against him. Still he loved those churches. My mother once said about her husband of fifty years, not meaning it as a compliment, "Your daddy gets me. He forgets every bad thing that ever happened to him in any church. He only remembers the good times and the good people. Why, he doesn't even remember which people were mean to him." Inadvertently, Mother paid Dad a great compliment. He taught his kids a great lesson. He just loved the churches, and no one was going to deprive him of wonderful memories about them.

At our house church came first. We lived by the maxim: If there is a church meeting, you are there. If we had a softball practice or a game on Wednesday evenings, we were in prayer meeting. If we got out in time, then we could take care of whatever else. Maybe that is one of the reasons I feel so at home standing in the pulpit; it beats trying to sit in a pew, watching the clock on the back wall in agonizing scrutiny and wondering if I am going to make the other meeting! But being in a church meeting and wanting it to hurry and end made a positive contribution to my preaching ministry: I only preach twenty to twenty-five minutes!

I listened to my dad preach from the pulpit in the church and then watched him live out his preaching during the week. I watched as he and Mother carefully laid aside their tithe every week. I heard their prayers. I heard them thank God for every sign of spiritual progress of church members, family, and friends. They always explained their love for the church. "If you love Christ, you will love his bride." They believed and lived out their belief that the church was not just an option; it was a necessity. Occasionally, when my Dad said I was going to do something, or refrain from doing something, I would say, "If I wasn't a preacher's kid, I would(n't) have to do this." My father always said with understanding, "Lynn, you are doing this because you are a preacher's kid. You are doing it because it is right, and you are doing it because you are a Christian."

I interviewed a wonderful young man who hit the game-winning home run in the College Baseball World Series in 1996. He was personable, polite, and humble. I watched him grow up in church and then watched as he maintained his Christian witness as a sports hero. In explaining his faith, he said, "Church was never an option in my home. If there was church, we knew where we would be." What a great testimony.

May all parents give their children the gift of speaking well of the church, supporting its causes, and attending its meetings.

Moral and Ethical Guidance

I struggled to keep silent, while showing strong interest. This was one of those moments for which a father prays, and I didn't want to mess it up. My son, in his mid-twenties, was talking about his plans for the future. He was talking about why he was going to do what he planned to do.

I promised myself I was going to listen, listen, listen, and not preach. And I did. I bit my tongue and never interrupted him. I was mighty proud of myself.

After mostly listening to his plans, I waited until he was completely finished and I could hold my tendencies no longer.

"Ron, I do not want to be presumptuous, but if you don't mind, I would like to respond to some of the things you have said." I was so proud of myself.

Ron, however, looked at me and said in all earnestness, "Dad, I don't want to hurt your feelings or to be rude, because I really do love you, but I know what you think."

Took my breath right away. I sat there silently for what seemed an hour and then forced a smile and said, "I guess you've heard it enough to know. Or maybe just enough."

Honestly, I don't think I could ask for more. Ron knows what I think. He knows how I feel. Now he is a grown man, with the right to make his own choices, accepting or rejecting what is precious to me. He is a bright, sweet young man of whom I am immensely proud. But we still disagree. I have struggled for years to approach him as a friend, knowing I can no longer force him or discipline him. Because I believe something is not a reason for Ron to believe it.

In my own life, I accepted and rejected some of my preacher father's beliefs. He made very sure I understood what he believed and expected. Gradually but surely, I had to make up my own mind on all these matters. On some things I agreed, and on some things I didn't. Didn't mean I loved my father any less nor appreciated his thoughts any less. I was able to separate loving him from accepting or rejecting his beliefs. In my better moments I grant my son the same privilege. I have great hope that he will surpass me, but he can't do that if he is tied to my level of thinking.

Unfortunately, lots of kids do not hear much from their parents about how to live. They receive more messages from the world. Wise parents will not let the world tell their kids what to do. They will not be silent. My parents, particularly my dad, certainly were not silent.

Any time my brother and I were riding along with Dad and we came to a prison, time permitting, Dad would pull into the prison parking lot and arrange an immediate tour of the facilities. In those days arranging such tours was not difficult. Most times we had a special tour with a guide and just the three of us. I'll have to admit, we toured some mighty interesting places, including execution chambers with readied electric chairs.

While we were touring the facilities, Dad would walk up to some unsuspecting inmate and start his series of questions: "Tell these boys how you ended up in here. Don't you wish you had done right so you wouldn't be in here? Did you think you would ever end up in a prison? Don't you wish you had minded your parents? Did you go to church?"

The startled inmate didn't know what to make of the entire situation, but he stammered out an answer. My dad probably got more confessions out of those men than the law officers and lawyers did at their trials! He wanted to make sure Paul and I realized we could end up there if we broke the law. Generally, the inmates wanted to do what they could to keep someone else from ending up behind bars.

Dad wanted to make absolutely certain my brother and I understood not only what was right and what was wrong, but what happened when one took things too far. He believed nothing beat firsthand testimonies.

Those tours may not have directly kept brother Paul and me from a life of crime, but they let us know what punishment for breaking the law was all about. A couple of times when I was with kids when they shoplifted a penny piece of candy or stole a watermelon from a field, I could feel those prison clothes creeping over my body or the straps of the electric chair being fastened on my arms and legs.

When I was a senior in high school, we lived in a small, two-bar town. (Bars were segregated by race.) My father was convinced that most of the ills of the world could be laid at the feet of drinking alcohol. A couple of times about midnight he loaded me into the family automobile and drove to one of the bars and parked across the street. For awhile we watched the comings and goings of the bar patrons. By that time of night, they were staggering in and out of the building. Dad would simply ask: "Would you like it if that were your father? How would you like it if that were your mother? Lynn, don't ever do that to your family. Don't live that kind of life."

Certainly Dad's choices of object lessons were not without fault and would not be without critics, but he let his kids know what he thought about the kind of lives he thought we would be wise to live. He would even turn the television set off when a beer or cigarette commercial came on. Imagine how thrilled he was when remote controls came along! His actions may have appeared silly to some, but it was his form of protest at some of the world's ills and his way of letting his kids know he thought alcohol and tobacco should have no place in our lives.

These were not the only ways my parents communicated ethics to me, but my folks certainly did want to impact my life for good. They wanted me to know that what we studied in church and in our daily Bible readings extended into all of life.

One thing for sure, you've got to get at this business of talking to your kids about right and wrong early-on. As soon as children are able to understand what is going on around them, they are besieged by messages from people trying to get them to do what they think is right. They sit in front of a television more than they sit in a classroom, and they spend more time at movies than they spend at church. Generally speaking, the messages of the media are presented strongly in entertaining, beautiful fashion—probably more appealing than a sermon or a lecture. The messages from television and movies about how to live are so warped, secular, and even anti-Christian, one shudders thinking about the effects they have on our children.

If these messages are the only ones our children receive, what are they to think? What will their values be? So, what can help counter these bombardments of messages? You—the parents.

Allow me to quote a study that will encourage you. The results of this 1995 study were published in the 1997 *Journal of the American Medical Association*. The federally funded study is the most comprehensive survey ever done of American adolescents and involved more than 12,000 students in grades 7-12. The bottom line of the story is this: The more teenagers feel loved by their parents and comfortable in their schools, the less likely they are to have early sex, smoke, abuse alcohol or drugs, or commit violence or suicide. That's on the prohibitive side. On the positive side, the researchers found that if parents expect adolescents to get good grades and refrain from sex, those expectations influence the adolescents' behavior powerfully through 12th grade, regardless of family income, race, or single- or dual-parent situations. Now that is encouraging!

Growing up, I lived in small towns. Usually, grades 1-12 were located in the same building. This meant all the classes started and ended at the same time. School buses and parents could make one run for all their kids, regardless of the ages. This meant further that parents could wake us all up at the same time, feed us all at the same time, and take us all to school at the same time.

This uniformity of schedules meant our family could have daily Bible readings every morning during the time we ate breakfast. Our denominational literature also gave us the names of foreign missionaries whose birthdays were on that date so we could pray for them.

Now, at times, morning devotions did not appear anything like some kind of worship. We kids fussed, and bickered, and moaned, and groaned. Our biggest complaint was that Dad always seemed to take too long getting the whole thing done. Dad was a preacher, and I think there were times he really enjoyed hearing himself read the Bible. He was good at noticing where the Bible reading began but terrible about noticing where he was supposed to stop. He would read on and on. One of us kids would dare ask, "Dad, are you sure you haven't read past the stopping place?" And then Dad would usually pray. I think he felt as if he could pray us little sermons for the day. For kids trying to get off to school, a minute seemed an hour, so it seemed we sat there for hours.

But I look back at those times and realize what genuine encouragements they were. I went about my day with the reminder that my life was not my own, and that I was not on my own. I appreciated those times as a youth, regardless of my protests. When I went off to college, I hungered for those times, and I searched to find another kind of Bible study group that could fill the gap of losing those moments at home.

I also benefited from my parents' wisdom and commitment at meal time. We actually ate together, at a regular table, sitting in chairs. We had a chrome and metal table with matching chrome and vinyl chairs. There we ate the greatest meals on earth. Mother never had to call the family to the table twice. There was no TV during this time, unless there was a particularly exciting football game on; Dad had a weakness for football. During mealtime we actually talked to each other. I heard my parents share their thoughts about all kinds of things—not just heavy stuff. But their spirit and attitudes seeped into me. I saw a better side of life, and it was good.

Since my kids were small, I have traveled a lot. I have always tried to take one of my youngsters with me if at all possible. That went for rather short driving trips as well as trips halfway around the world. On these trips they became sort of a captive audience. Ron or Stephanie and I had wonderful opportunities to share our thoughts with very little interruption. What wonderful times!

When Ron was about five years old, I took him on a photography assignment hours from home. I had my professional cameras, and he had a Point-and-Shoot Polaroid. I shot my photos, and he shot his.

We went to a farm in Nebraska to cover a family there. My son was a city boy and had never spent the night on a farm of any kind, much less a remote one like that. We had a great supper and a wonderful visit with the family, and then they showed us to our upstairs bedroom. The house was a very old farmstead house with no central heating. When the family went to bed, all lights and heat went off. Our bed for the night was covered with handmade quilts. When we got into bed, the quilts were so heavy, if I lay on my back, they mashed my toes down. And it was dark, dark, dark. The winds and snow were blowing across that open, expansive plain. The old house was squeaking and groaning. I wondered how my city boy was fairing there beside me, but I just lay there silently to see what he would say. Finally, he spoke.

"Daddy, which way are you facing?"

"I'm facing the wall."

"Daddy, if you don't mind, would you turn over and sleep facing me tonight?"

He wanted to feel the reassurance that his dad was looking after him.

Children need to know their parents care about them and about how they live. They need to hear frequent reassurances of what we expect and what we believe is right and wrong. If we do not let them know the kind of life we expect them to live, they will believe the silence gives consent to all the other messages they are hearing. We must seek to let them know we care about them and love them as they do their best to do right. Of course, they will think we are old-fashioned, but they will know what we think. And as they get older, they will appreciate the gift of moral and ethical guidance more and more.

I am thankful my father and mother gave me the mechanisms to make decisions and pointed me toward what they based their faith upon and said is a destination worth living. Gradually, they let me go, set me free to make my own decisions and seek my own destination. The older I get, the more I'm grateful.

Gifts that Touch the Soul

My dad was at my home during Christmas week when we received news of a malignant, inoperable brain tumor. The doctors gave him only a few months to live. The tumor dulled Dad's thinking, but he still had some real flashes of insight. We tried radiation, but it only exploded the growth of the tumor. Mother and I decided the treatment should be discontinued.

Dad faced death with incredible faith and courage. When we stopped the treatment, Dad said to me the next day, "Son, they've stopped the treatment. Was the radiation making 'that thing' grow?"

"Yes, Daddy. I'm sorry, but that is what happened."

"That means I'm going to die soon."

Tears burned in my eyes. My throat choked. I never thought I would have to tell my father he was going to die. How could I do it?

"Yes, Daddy. I'm afraid so."

There was a long time of silence.

"What are you thinking, Daddy?"

"I'm thinking about dying."

"What do you think about it?"

"Well, I don't mind dying. It just seems like such a shame to go off and leave such a wonderful family."

A pause.

"I don't mind dying," he smiled. "I just hate dying in Alexandria, Louisiana!"

(It wasn't that he hated Alexandria so much—he just hated being separated from his wonderful friends in Wichita, Kansas, where he had ministered some twenty years.)

The next day Daddy called me to his side and placed something in my hand.

"Lynn, I want you to have this. Don't give it to anyone, and don't sell it."

I looked in my hand, and there was a diamond ring.

"Dad, you keep it."

"No, I want you to have it. You are my preacher-boy. You keep it."

Daddy was a child of poverty before the Great Depression of the 1930s came along and made things worse. He never moaned or groaned about the grinding hardships of life, but from time to time he did recount various things he and his family did to survive those hard days.

My father's income never exceeded what is considered lower-middle or working-class. Therefore, I never understood why later in life, when he got all of his children out of the house and had the opportunity to spend money on other things, he bought a diamond ring. It was not a small ring, and it was not a small diamond. It cost several thousand dollars.

I asked him why he bought it. He told me what his father told him: "Son, buy a diamond ring when you can. You will enjoy wearing it. And as long as you have it, you will not be broke." That sounds sort of silly to folks born later, but I learned a number of other men Dad's age had heard the same words and followed that advice.

I put the ring in the safest place I could imagine and left it there for months, unable to wear it.

"Lynn, where is your daddy's ring?" Mother asked one day.

"I just haven't been able to wear it."

"Lynn, your daddy gave you that ring to wear. You get it out and wear it."

So I did. I never had such a mixture of appreciation, pride, and sadness.

That night I wore the ring to a basketball game where my daughter was cheerleading. I went to the restroom and took the ring off and placed it on the lavatory while I washed my hands. Someone spoke to me, and I turned to talk. We walked out of the restroom together. Ten yards outside the door I realized I had left the ring on the lavatory.

I rushed back to the lavatory, but the ring was gone. I searched and advertised and asked and begged, but I never saw the ring again. It was gone. Lost. The most financially precious thing my father had, he gave to me, and I lost it. My body aches with pain even now.

But thank God, the most precious gifts my father and mother gave to me, I cannot lose. Those gifts touched my soul. They grow more precious every day. I appreciate them more than ever before, and I know I will appreciate them more tomorrow.

What will it prosper you if you give your children the whole world, but do not give them gifts that touch their souls?